Buttons and the Big Squeeze

A true story about a little dog who never gave up

Written by Nancy Bond

Illustrated by Emily Lux

Hedgehog Press
An imprint of Story Bridges Press
Oakland, CA

ISBN Hardcover 978-0-9887631-5-9

Cover Design by Emily Lux
Book Design by Uniquely Perfect
www.uniquelyperfect.com

Printed in the United States of America

The paper used in this publication meets the minium requirements of American National Standard for Information Sciences—Permanence of Paper for Printed Library Materials, ANSI/NISO X39-48-1992.

To the people in my family
who inspire me
by their "never give up" attitude

Buttons pranced happily along beside Cole as they skipped along the dirt road going up to the high pasture.

The day was sunny and warm.

Buttons was hoping he could play with the rabbit family, who would be out scampering around the rocky pasture.

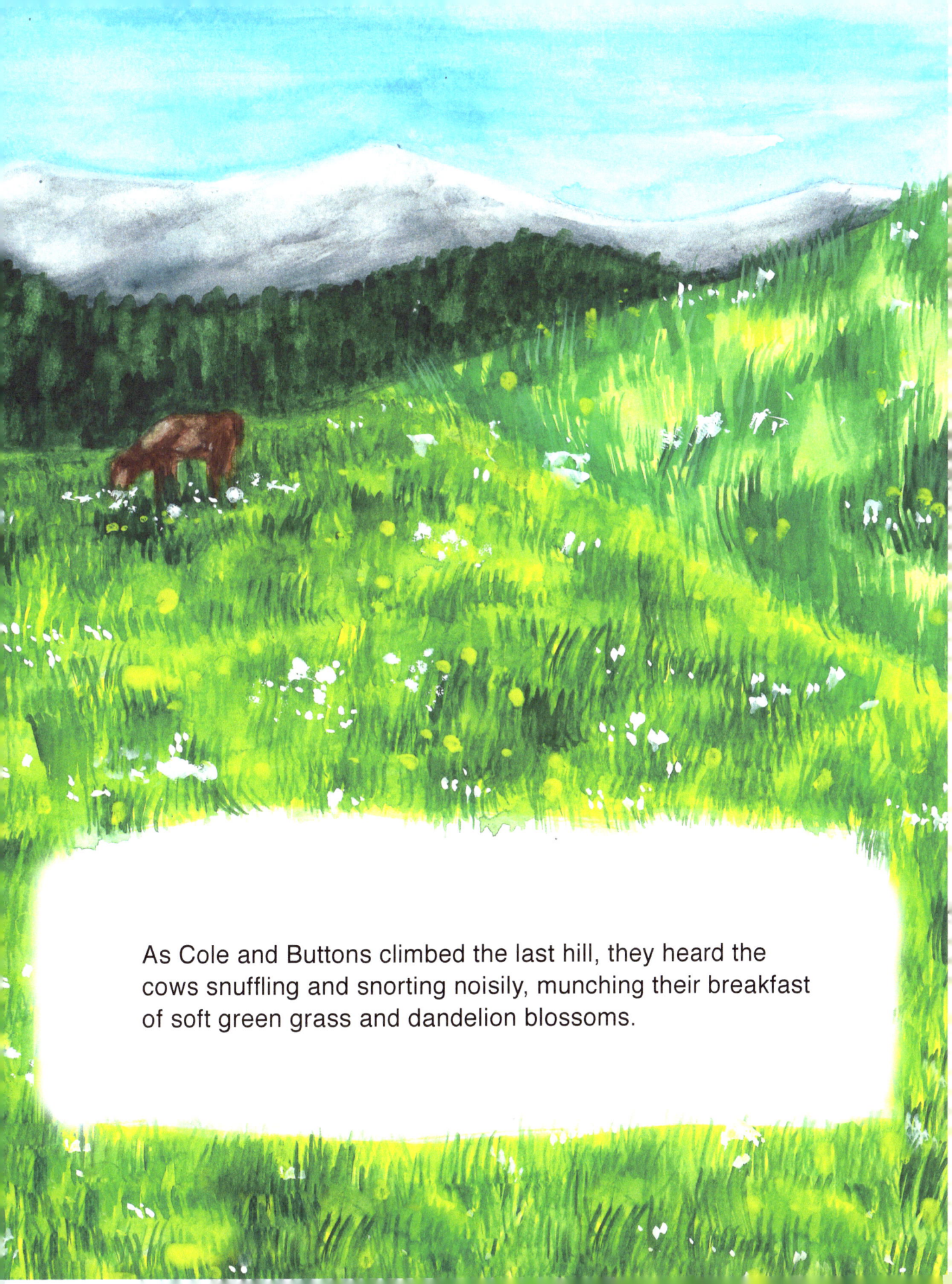

As Cole and Buttons climbed the last hill, they heard the cows snuffling and snorting noisily, munching their breakfast of soft green grass and dandelion blossoms.

Suddenly Buttons' sharp eyes caught sight of his friends, the rabbits, racing around the rocks further up the hill, playing tag and squealing excitedly.

"Here I am!" Buttons barked, "I want to play, too."

He raced off to join the noisy, hopping group. He was amazed when they all disappeared.

"Wait," he cried, "wait for me!"

He ran to the nearest rabbit hole, put his nose inside, and began to dig.

Soon he dug the hole just big enough for his plump little stomach and then he wiggled and squirmed down further and further.

His strong front legs pulled forward, his back legs pushed, and he was a long way into the ground as he continued to bark, "Rabbit, Rabbit, wait up!"

There was no answer at all so after sniffing the tunnel air a few more times, Buttons decided to go back home and come back another day.

RABBIT

WAIT UP!!!

Cole's calls sounded very far away. "Buttons, Buttons, come on—let's go!"

But when Buttons tried to back out, he discovered he couldn't move. The more he wiggled the more the dirt fell around him.

At last he became too tired to try anymore. "This is a really big squeeze but I'll never give up. I'll try again tomorrow," he decided.

He rested his nose on his front paws.

"Never again," he thought to himself, "never, never again will I play with rabbits."

He moved his nose further down on his paws and fell asleep.

He awoke to a wiggly nose touching his own dirt covered nose. Rabbit was trying to climb out of his tunnel entrance into the morning sun. "You're in my way, Dog," he squeaked unhappily.

"Well, I don't want to be here either," whined Buttons.

"Can you help me back up?"

"No, I can't, and this is very inconsiderate of you," Rabbit snapped, as he easily turned around and scampered back the way he had come.

Buttons watched helplessly as Rabbit disappeared into the dark tunnel.

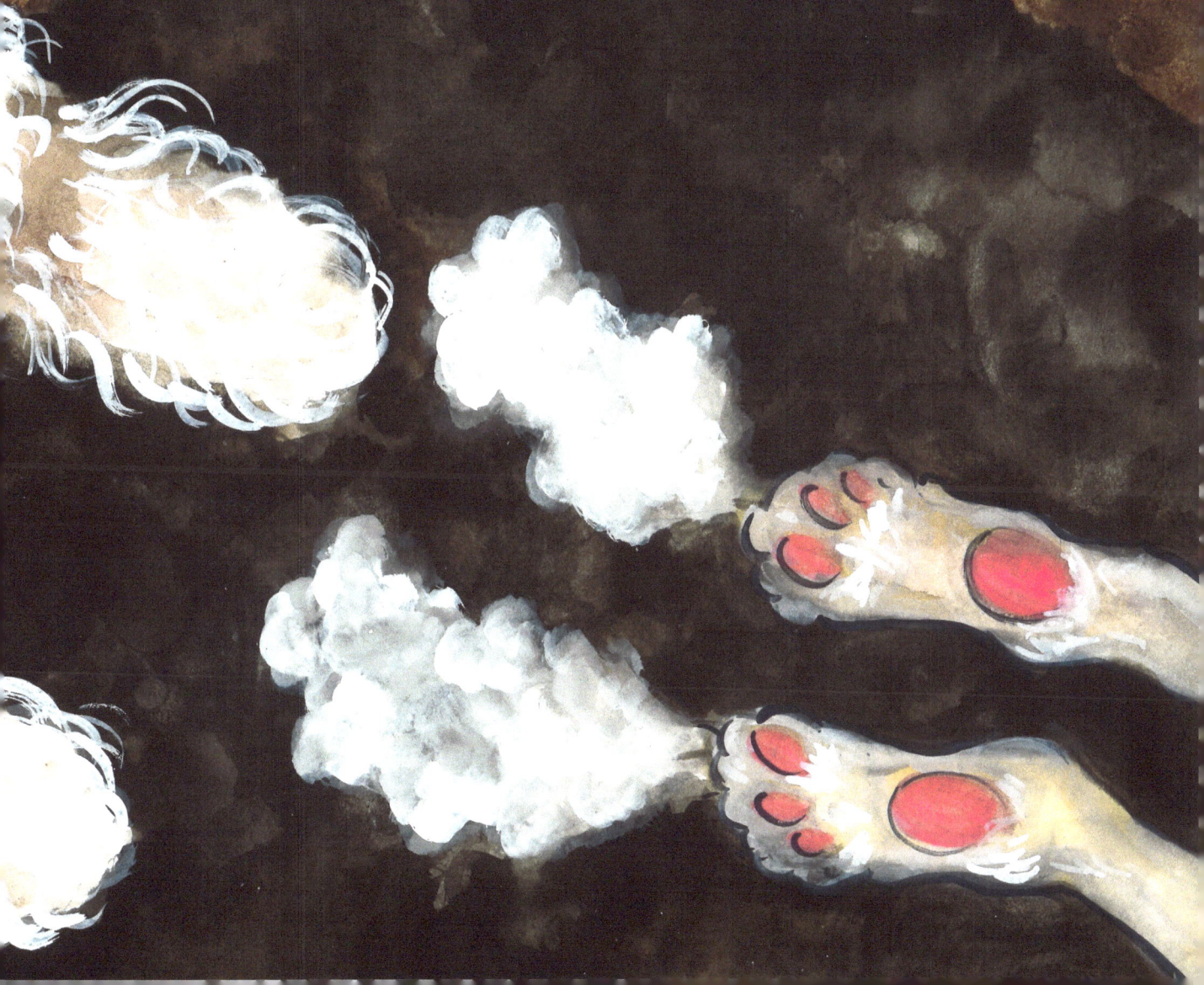

Buttons lay there whimpering all day, and the next day, and the next. Each day he tried to back up but his little body just wouldn't budge.

After each wiggle and push, he thought, "I'll never give up. I'll try again tomorrow."

Buttons was all alone except for the earthworms that popped through the sides and top of the tunnel. They stared at him in surprise and alarm.

"Oh, my goodness! This will never do. How did you manage to get in here?"

Then, without waiting for Buttons to answer, they quickly pulled back and disappeared.

Every day Cole came up the hill and called for Buttons.

When there was no answering bark, Cole always said to himself, "I'll never give up. I'll try again tomorrow."

On the fourth day Rabbit returned.

When he looked into Buttons' sad black button eyes he sighed in disgust.

"Try to back up, will you? I'm tired of using my emergency exit all the time."

He hunched on his hind legs, crossed his forepaws and tapped one foot impatiently.

Buttons wiggled around and there did seem to be a little more room in the rabbit hole.

He was definitely feeling hungry.

He noticed Rabbit stayed just out of reach down the tunnel.

Another cold, miserable night went by as Buttons dreamed of delicious dog food, scrumptious, crunchy bones, and his cozy warm bed at home.

When he awoke he felt there really was more room in the tunnel.

With all the strength he had left he began to push backward.

"I think I'm moving," he panted hopefully.

He pushed backward for a long time and then...

"I think I feel the sun on my tail! Maybe one more BIG push..."

With one last frantic wiggle, his entire skinny body popped out onto the grassy pasture and into the warm morning sunshine.

The curious cows stopped chewing and snorted at him in surprise.

He blinked in the bright sunlight and shook the rabbit hole dirt off his fur.

Way off in the distance he could hear Cole calling, "Buttons, Buttons, are you there? Come on Buttons! Bone, Buttons, bone!"

BUTTONS AR

YOU THERE?

Buttons barked a short, excited bark, "I'm coming, I'm coming, wait for me!"

Off he ran, his wobbly legs propelling him down the hill toward home.

He ran to where they were calling him and where his food dish was and his nice, smelly bed.

Down the hill to Cole, who loved him and played with him.

"I'm glad I never gave up," he woofed to himself.

"No more playing with Rabbit. His house is way too dark and he doesn't play nice."

Back on the hillside, Rabbit watched Buttons leap into Cole's arms.

Then with a sniff he turned back to his hole and began housecleaning.

He pushed out all the dirt that smelled like dog and carefully picked up all of Buttons' hairs.

When he looked at the huge hole Buttons had made, he sighed.

"This just won't do at all. Its's so big the fox could even visit. I'll have to dig another home right away. How bothersome is that!"

Then he shook his head in disgust. "I just hope he doesn't come back here and try to play anymore. Never again. Never, never again."

And he didn't. Buttons was very happy in his own home where he could lie in the sun, eat whenever he wanted from his own food bowl, and cuddle in bed with his best friend, Cole.

Buttons never ran off looking for the rabbit family again.

Up on the hill the rabbits played their rabbit games alone and the cows roamed around munching peacefully, grateful that no dog interrupted their breakfast anymore.

Buttons sat in the soft green grass by his doghouse with his bowl of fresh water and a new bone beside him.

He was very contented but he just couldn't resist one more look up the hill, remembering his adventure.

"I never gave up," he woofed softly, "but no more rabbits. Never again, never, never again!"

ABOUT THE BOOK: I remember Buttons the wire haired terrier. He was the bouncing little bundle of energy my parents lived with, bringing delight, love and laughter into their lives. Buttons was curious, eager, fearless, and loved chasing rabbits, squirrels, and any other small thing that ran.They all lived in the eastern Oregon town of Baker, on a ranch with lots of running room.

While out with them on an evening stroll Buttons went exploring over the hilly pasture, off on his own adventure, and they had to return home without him. Unexpectedly, he didn't return to the farmhouse and over the course of four or five days they searched and called but, sadly, he was nowhere to be found. A week went by and then one morning he turned up barking and scratching at the door. He was very thin, very thirsty, and very dirty. They think he chased an animal into it's burrow, became wedged in deeply and couldn't budge until he was thin enough to back out.

He recovered well and lived happily ever after, gnawing bones and staying home. He had just plain lost any interest in chasing rabbits and squirrels, recalling, no doubt, his dark, lonely and hungry days underground.

www.ingramcontent.com/pod-product-compliance
Lightning Source LLC
Chambersburg PA
CBHW042012080426
42734CB00002B/61